Comets

by Gregory L. Vogt

Consultant:
Ralph Winrich
Former NASA Aerospace Education Specialist

Bridgestone Books
an imprint of Capstone Press
Mankato, Minnesota

Bridgestone Books are published by Capstone Press
151 Good Counsel Drive, P.O. Box 669, Mankato, Minnesota 56002
http://www.capstone-press.com

Library of Congress Cataloging-in-Publication Data
Vogt, Gregory.
    Comets / by Gregory L. Vogt.
    p. cm.—(The galaxy)
    Includes bibliographical references and index.
    Summary: Describes the formation, exploration, and parts of a comet, including how
people have perceived comets throughout history.
    ISBN 0-7368-1119-2
    1. Comets—Juvenile literature. [1. Comets.] I. Title. II. Series.
QB721.5 .V66 2002
523.6—dc21
    2001003090

Editorial Credits

Tom Adamson, editor; Karen Risch, product planning editor; Timothy Halldin,
    cover designer and interior layout designer; Jenny Schonborn, interior illustrator and
    production designer; Katy Kudela, photo researcher

Photo Credits

Astronomical Society of the Pacific, cover, 1, 20
Bill and Sally Fletcher/TOM STACK & ASSOCIATES, 8, 12
Gustav Verderber/Visuals Unlimited, 4
Photo Network, 16
Rick Scott and Joe Orman, 14
StockTrek/PhotoDisc/PictureQuest, 6, 10, 18

1 2 3 4 5 6 07 06 05 04 03 02

Table of Contents

What Are Comets?

A comet is a ghostly looking object in the night sky. It first appears as a faint fuzzy patch. Each night it becomes larger and brighter. A tail forms that points away from the Sun. A comet is one of the rarer objects in the solar system. The solar system is the Sun and everything that moves around it.

A comet's center is made of ice, snow, and rock. The center is called the nucleus. A giant cloud of gas forms around the nucleus. Comet nuclei are usually just a few miles or kilometers wide.

The nucleus travels around the Sun in a very long orbit shaped like a stretched-out circle. This shape is called an ellipse. The nucleus usually is very far from the Sun. The nucleus becomes visible when it moves near the Sun. The Sun's warmth melts some of the ice. Gas and dust stream off the nucleus. The tail can stretch for 10 million miles (16 million kilometers) or more across space.

People could see comet Hale-Bopp from the ground in 1997.

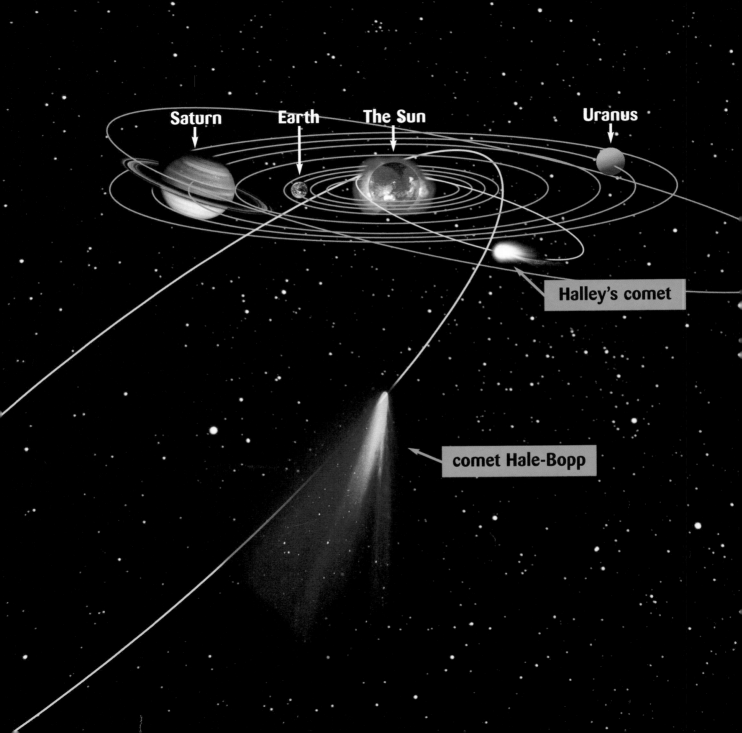

Saturn

Earth

The Sun

Uranus

Halley's comet

comet Hale-Bopp

How Are Comets Formed?

Comets are ancient. Astronomers think that comets are leftovers from when the solar system formed.

The solar system began more than 5 billion years ago. It formed from a huge cloud of gas and dust. Gravity caused most of that matter to come together in the cloud's center. This created the Sun.

Smaller clumps of matter collected together and began swirling around the Sun. These clumps formed the planets and moons. The leftovers became comet nuclei and asteroids. Asteroids are made of rock and metal. They can be up to a few hundred miles or kilometers across.

Comet nuclei probably formed between the orbits of the planets Saturn and Uranus. It was cooler there than in the middle of the solar system. Water, rock, and dust froze together into trillions of comet nuclei. The planets collided with some of the nuclei. The giant planets pushed other nuclei out into distant orbits.

Comet nuclei probably formed between the orbits of Saturn and Uranus. The sizes of the Sun, planets, and comets are not to scale in this illustration.

The nucleus of a comet looks like a very large and dirty snowball. Some comet nuclei are icy. Others are made up of fluffy snow.

The ice and snow start to melt when the comet is near the Sun. The snow turns into gas. Dust and rock are released into space as the snow and ice melt. The dust and gas shoot outward. This creates a large ball of gas and dust around the nucleus called the coma. The coma is the head of the comet. A coma can be 1,000 times larger than the nucleus.

The Sun allows people to see the coma. Particles of light from the Sun strike the coma. The particles push gas and dust behind the coma. The gas and dust stretch out to become a long tail.

The coma is the head of a comet. The tail streams behind the coma away from the Sun.

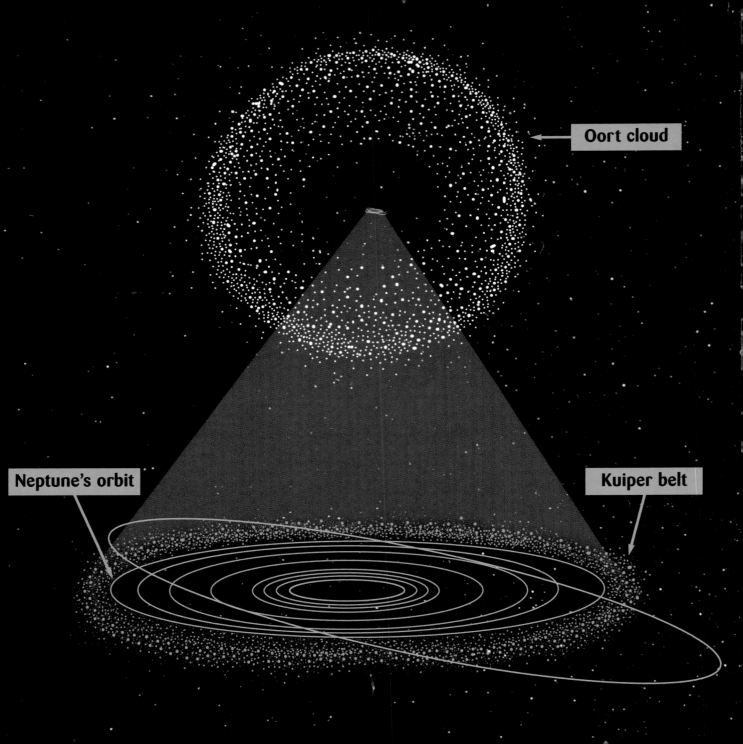

Throughout history, only a few thousand comets have been discovered. Astronomers think there are trillions of comet nuclei in the solar system. The nuclei stay far away from the Sun in a place called the Oort cloud. This cloud is like a huge shell surrounding the solar system. The inner edge of the shell is 20,000 times farther away from the Sun than Earth is. The outer edge is 100,000 times farther away.

A star sometimes passes near the Oort cloud. The star's gravity changes the orbits of some of the nuclei. They start falling toward the Sun. People eventually can see these nuclei as comets.

Other comet nuclei orbit the Sun in a zone called the Kuiper belt. This area is located beyond the orbit of the planet Neptune. Astronomers think there may be a billion comet nuclei in the Kuiper belt.

The top illustration shows where the Oort cloud may be. The Kuiper belt is just beyond Neptune's orbit.

A Comet's Orbit

When a comet leaves the Oort cloud, it moves to the inner solar system. The comet may fall into the Sun and be destroyed. Or the comet may pass near Jupiter. The planet's gravity will change the comet's orbit.

A coma forms first as the nucleus approaches the Sun. Sunlight then blows some of the gas behind the nucleus to form a tail.

Comets can have one or two tails. The ion tail is made of gases. This straight blue-white tail points directly away from the Sun. The other kind of tail is made of dust. Dust tails look white and often are curved.

After passing around the Sun, the comet heads back into deep space. The tail still points away from the Sun. Gradually, the nucleus gets colder and the ice stops melting. The last of the gas and dust disappear into space, making the comet invisible again.

A comet's ion tail points directly away from the Sun. The dust tail often is curved.

Comet Dust

A comet leaves a dirty trail through space. It releases dust and sand grains as its nucleus melts. These particles travel around the Sun in the same path as the nucleus.

In time, the comet's entire orbit becomes a thin belt of dust and sand. The particles are too small and spread apart to be seen from Earth. But people can see them at certain times. Earth sometimes passes through the orbit of a comet. When this happens, some of the comet particles collide with Earth's atmosphere.

The comet dust and sand travel very fast through space. These particles get very hot when they strike Earth's atmosphere. They rub against the gases in the atmosphere. This rubbing causes the particles to heat up and burn. They become fast-moving, bright streaks across the night sky. The streaks are called meteors.

This meteor was caused by a dust particle from the orbit of comet Swift-Tuttle.

FAST FACTS: Some Famous Comets

Name	Year Discovered	Last Appearance	Next Appearance	Orbit Length
Halley	240 B.C.	1986	2061	76.01 years
Brorsen-Metcalf	1847	1989	2059	70.54 years
Swift-Tuttle	1862	1992	2126	135 years
Giacobini-Zinner	1900	1998	2005	6.61 years
Taylor	1915	1997	2004	6.97 years
Schwassmann-Wachmann 1	1927	1989	2004	14.85 years
Whipple	1933	1994	2003	8.53 years
Bowell-Skiff	1983	1999	2015	16.18 years
Shoemaker-Levy 4	1991	1997	2003	6.51 years
Hale-Bopp	1995	1997	4377	changes

Comets in History

Few comets are bright enough for people to see without a telescope. Bright comets only appear every few years.

Long ago, some people thought comets were hairy stars. Others thought comets were warnings of bad things to come. People blamed comets for fires, floods, earthquakes, and volcanic eruptions. But comets did not cause the disasters.

Two thousand years ago, a Greek named Aristotle thought comets were burning patches of air. In the 1400s, astronomer Tycho Brahe used angle-measuring tools to study a comet. He learned that the comet was not a part of Earth's atmosphere. Instead, he showed that comets were many times farther away than the Moon.

One of the most famous comets is Halley's comet. It was first seen by Chinese astronomers in 240 B.C.

Halley's comet returns to the inner solar system every 76 years.

Halley's Comet

In 1705, English astronomer Edmond Halley studied the records of different comets. People thought that three different comets had appeared in 1531, 1607, and 1682. Halley realized it was a single comet with a 76-year orbit. He said that the comet would return in 1758. He was right. The comet was named in his honor.

More recently, Halley's comet appeared in 1910 and 1986. The 1910 passage caused an uproar. Earth's orbit passed through the tail of the comet. Many people sealed themselves in their homes so they would not breathe the comet's gases. But nothing happened because the gas in the tail is very thin.

A group of space probes studied Halley's comet when it appeared in 1986. The space probe *Giotto* took close-up pictures. Halley's nucleus is about 9 miles (14 kilometers) long and 5 miles (8 kilometers) wide. The surface is covered with a dark crust.

Astronomers expect Halley's comet to return to the inner solar system again in 2061.

piece of comet
Shoemaker-Levy 9

The Death of a Comet

A comet becomes smaller each time it passes near the Sun. Space probes studying Halley's comet measured how much matter was lost. About 1 yard (1 meter) of ice evaporated from Halley's nucleus while it was warmed by the Sun. A comet eventually melts away after many passes by the Sun.

Some comets head directly into the Sun. The comet is destroyed as it enters the solar atmosphere. Other comets strike planets. In 1908, a small comet struck Earth near Siberia. The nucleus exploded before the comet could reach the ground. The blast flattened trees up to 20 miles (32 kilometers) away.

In 1992, comet Shoemaker-Levy 9 passed near Jupiter. Jupiter's gravity broke the comet's nucleus into at least 21 smaller pieces. The pieces were flung out into space. Two years later, the pieces fell back and collided with Jupiter. Each piece exploded in Jupiter's atmosphere. Jupiter had dark blotches in its upper atmosphere for many days.

Pieces of comet Shoemaker-Levy 9 left dark blotches on Jupiter for many days.

Hands On: Draw a Comet's Orbit

The orbit of a comet looks like a stretched-out circle. This shape is called an ellipse. The Sun is located at one end of the orbit. The other end of the orbit is in deep space.

What You Need

Pencil or pen
Sheet of paper
Ruler

Piece of cardboard
2 push tacks
String

What You Do

1. Draw a straight line down the middle of the paper. Place an X at the halfway point on the line.
2. On the line, measure 1 inch (2.5 centimeters) away from the X in both directions. Place a dot at each spot.
3. With the cardboard underneath the paper, push the tacks through the dots.
4. Tie a 6-inch (15-centimeter) loop of string. Lay it around the tacks. Put the tip of the pen or pencil inside the loop. Pull the loop snug as you draw a curved line around the tacks.

You have drawn an ellipse. This is the shape of a comet's orbit. The Sun would be located where one of the tacks is. Look at how the orbit is different from a circle. What would happen if you moved the tacks farther apart? Closer together?

Words to Know

astronomer (uh-STRON-uh-mer)—a person who studies planets, stars, and space

coma (KOH-muh)—the head of a comet

dust tail (DUHST TAYL)—a long stream of comet dust pointing away from the Sun; this white tail often is curved.

gravity (GRAV-uh-tee)—a force that pulls objects together

ion tail (EYE-on TAYL)—a long stream of comet gas pointing away from the Sun; this blue-white tail is always straight.

meteor (MEE-tee-ur)—a streak of light in the sky caused by a piece of rock or dust that enters Earth's atmosphere

nucleus (NOO-klee-uhss)—the lump of ice, snow, rock, and dust that moves around the Sun; a nucleus forms into a comet when it is warmed by the Sun.

orbit (OR-bit)—the path of an object as it moves around another object in space

Read More

Bonar, Samantha. *Comets.* A First Book. New York: Franklin Watts, 1998.

Gallant, Roy A. *Comets, Asteroids, and Meteorites.* Kaleidoscope. Tarrytown, N.Y.: Benchmark Books, 2001.

Kerrod, Robin. *Asteroids, Comets, and Meteors.* Planet Library. Minneapolis: Lerner, 2000.

Useful Addresses

Canadian Space Agency
6767 Route de l'Aéroport
Saint-Hubert, QC J3Y 8Y9
Canada

NASA Headquarters
Washington, DC 20546-0001

Internet Sites

Cometography.com
http://cometography.com
The Nine Planets—Comets
· http://www.staq.qld.edu.au/k9p/comets.htm
StarChild
http://starchild.gsfc.nasa.gov/docs/StarChild/StarChild.html

Index